# Everybody Digs Soil

# SOIL EROSION AND HOW TO PREVENT IT

## Natalie Hyde

Crabtree Publishing Company
www.crabtreebooks.com

# Crabtree Publishing Company

www.crabtreebooks.com

**Author:** Natalie Hyde
**Editor-in-Chief:** Lionel Bender
**Editor:** Lynn Peppas
**Project coordinator:** Kathy Middleton
**Photo research:** Susannah Jayes
**Designer:** Ben White
**Production coordinator:** Ken Wright
**Production:** Kim Richardson
**Prepress technician:** Ken Wright

**Consultant:** Heather L. Montgomery, children's writer, environmental educator, and science education consultant who runs Dragonfly Programs: http://www.dragonflyeeprograms.com

**Cover:** Roots help anchor plants in the ground and hold soil in place, preventing erosion.

**Title page:** A view of the Grand Canyon, created by weathering and erosion.

This book was produced for Crabtree Publishing Company by Bender Richardson White

**Photographs and reproductions:**
Dreamstime: cover (girl watering tree)
© FLPA: pages 7 left (Thomas Marent/Minden Pictures), 8 (ImageBroker), 11 left (Nigel Cattlin), 17 left (Winfried Wisniewski), 21 right (Konrad Wothe/Minden Pictures), 28 (Mike J Thomas)
© Getty Images: pages 4/5 (Rich Wheater), 14/15 (AFP/Getty Images), 16/17 (AFP/Getty Images), 20, 21 left (Jason Edwards), 24 (AFP/Getty Images), 26 (Angelo Cavalli)
© iStockphoto.com: Headline image (redmal), pages 4 (Wojtek Kryczka), 5 (redmal), 6 (Eric Foltz), 7 right (Victor Makhankov), 9 left (misokaco), 9 right (Ian Hubball), 13 left (Frank van den Bergh), 13 right (wrangel), 15 right (Luther Zimmerman), 18 (Greg Gardner), 19 right (Bart Coenders), 22 (Peeter Viisimaa), 22/23 (Robert Koopmans), 23 (Dennis Guyitt), 25 left (Brian Palmer), 25 right (Ryan Thompson), 27 left (Darryl Sleath), 29 left (Nina Shannon), 29 right (ranplett)
© www.shutterstock.com: cover (all except girl watering tree), title page and pages 10/11 (Albo), 11 right (Lee Torrens), 12 (Kondrachov Vladimir), 19 left (SergioZ)
© Topfoto: page 15 (Lightroom Photos/NASA)
USDA Natural Resources Conservation Service: pages 17 right, 27 right

**Library and Archives Canada Cataloguing in Publication**

Hyde, Natalie, 1963-
    Soil erosion and how to prevent it / Natalie Hyde.

(Everybody digs soil)
Includes index.
ISBN 978-0-7787-5403-9 (bound).--ISBN 978-0-7787-5416-9 (pbk.)

    1. Soil erosion--Juvenile literature. I. Title. II. Series: Everybody digs soil

S623.3.H93 2010          j631.4'5          C2009-906275-5

**Library of Congress Cataloging-in-Publication Data**

Hyde, Natalie, 1963-
 Soil erosion and how to prevent it / Natalie Hyde.
    p. cm. -- (Everybody digs soil)
Includes index.
 ISBN 978-0-7787-5416-9 (pbk. : alk. paper) -- ISBN 978-0-7787-5403-9 (reinforced library binding : alk. paper)
 1. Soil erosion--Juvenile literature. I. Title.

 S623.3.H93 2010
 631.4'5--dc22
                                                    2009042782

# Crabtree Publishing Company

www.crabtreebooks.com          1-800-387-7650

Printed in the U.S.A./122009/BG20090930

**Published in Canada**
**Crabtree Publishing**
616 Welland Ave.
St. Catharines, Ontario
L2M 5V6

**Published in the United States**
**Crabtree Publishing**
PMB 59051
350 Fifth Avenue, 59th Floor
New York, New York 10118

**Published in the United Kingdom**
**Crabtree Publishing**
Maritime House
Basin Road North, Hove
BN41 1WR

**Published in Australia**
**Crabtree Publishing**
386 Mt. Alexander Rd.
Ascot Vale (Melbourne)
VIC 3032

# CONTENTS

# THE VALUE OF SOIL

The hard rocky surface of Earth is covered with an amazing material. It is a layer of crushed rocks and **organic**, or nature-made, material called soil. Soil is only a thin layer but it is vital for life on our planet.

## MOVING AROUND

Soil does not always stay in one place. Wind, water, and ice carry soil from one place to another. This is called **erosion**. Erosion is a natural process but humans can cause erosion, too. Without enough soil, an area can become empty of plant and animal life. This can mean the difference between humans having enough food to eat and starvation.

▶ *Soil itself is made up of layers. Plants grow in topsoil, the uppermost layer.*

## SOIL AND FOOD

✱ Soil is home to millions of life forms. Many of them are tiny, such as **bacteria** and types of fungi, algae, and simple animals. This micro life is necessary to process **nutrients**, or food materials, in the soil and make them available for plants. All animals depend on plants, either by eating them directly or by feeding on plant-eaters. Plants are the beginning of all food chains or feeding networks.

## CLEANING UP

Soil also works as a storage system and water filter. As rainwater seeps down through soil, some of it gets trapped between the particles, or tiny pieces, of soil. There, it is stored until used by soil creatures and plants, or it disappears as the soil dries out. Anything floating in the water is also trapped by the soil. The deeper the water goes, the more floating material is removed. The water that reaches rock beneath the soil is clean and clear. The clean water flows downhill in streams.

◄ *A plant's root network spreads through soil.*

## DEEP DOWN

Roots help anchor plants in the ground. Roots also hold soil in place. Without the root systems of trees, bushes, **crops**, and other plants, soil is easily eroded. Rainfall and gravity—the force that pulls everything downward—can cause **landslides** and mudslides, endangering villages and towns.

◄ *Soil starts life as rock. It forms over thousands of years.*

# HOW SOIL IS MADE

▼ *Rock-climbing*

The surface of Earth is always changing. **Mountain building** and volcanoes raise and break up the land. Water, wind, and ice wear it down again.

## ROCK-BREAKING

As soon as new rock is formed, weather begins breaking it down. Big bits of rock break off and fall or are carried downhill by streams, winds, or **glaciers**. The big rocks become smaller. Eventually a layer of pebbles, stones, gravel, and **minerals** gathers. Minerals contain chemicals that we use, such as metals, and those that are nutrients for life forms.

## SOIL FACTS

✳ It can take 3,000 to 12,000 years to make soil **mature**, or rich enough in nutrients, for farming. Soil develops faster in areas that are warm and wet rather than cold and dry.

*▶ Earthworms in soil.*

## LIFE-FORMS APPEAR

✳ Mosses and **lichens** are usually the first **organisms**, or living things, to grow on a rocky surface. They attract micro life that decomposes, or breaks down, any living things that die. The organic material they create—known as humus—makes it possible for other plants to grow. The plants attract soil animals such as worms and insects. Their body wastes add to the organic material. Eventually a thick covering of soil forms.

## SOIL HELPERS

Creatures that live under ground also help build up soil. Insects shred and tear apart dead leaves and stems. Earthworms and ants moving through the soil transport material from the surface down deep into the ground.

## ON THE MOVE

Soil that is made mostly of sand or **silt** erodes more quickly than clay-rich soil. Particles of sand and silt are much bigger than those of clay. They are more easily blown or washed away. Sand dunes in the desert can be blown as much as 165 feet (50 m) in a day.

*◀ Water flowing downhill carries with it grains of all sizes, shapes, and colors.*

# WASTING AWAY

The Earth's surface is not flat. There are hills and slopes everywhere. Some are covered with small plants and trees and others are bare. Gravity can pull down the material from these uplands slowly and gently or fast and dangerously.

▼ Landslide damage

## LANDSLIDES

✳ Landslides start when soil and rocks at the top of a slope are loosened. Then gravity takes over. As the rocks and soil begin to slide down, they pick up speed. Boulders, trees, and anything else in the way get pushed along. People or buildings that are in the way are also in danger. When there is a loss of life or damage to property, the landslide is called a natural disaster.

Naturel
Cafe & Patisserie

## IMPORTANT ROOTS

Plants of all sizes help keep soil in place. Their roots are like a net or web holding everything together. When trees and shrubs are removed, soil and rocks become **unstable**. Rainwater that is not taken up by roots fills air pockets in the ground. This turns soil to mud, which slides more easily. Mudslides can roar down slopes at more than 35 miles per hour (56 km/h).

◄ *Cutting down trees can allow soil to erode.*

## WEATHERING

Wind, water, and big changes in temperature all help to break down rocks. This is called **weathering**. Rocks and soil that are not covered by trees and other plants have no protection from these forces. The ground in these areas is weathered and weakened more quickly. Water running off this land forms **gulleys**, or huge channels, in the ground.

▲ *Erosion can happen easily after weathering occurs.*

# EROSION BY WATER

The most powerful force of erosion in nature is running water. Over time, streams can cut channels or tunnels into solid rock. They also carry away huge amounts of soil and rock particles.

▼ The Grand Canyon was carved by water.

## CARVING THE EARTH'S SURFACE

Not all rocks are hard. Some, such as limestone and sandstone, can be eroded by rainwater. Where soft rock lies between hard rock, the water can wear away a V-shaped groove or channel in the soft rock. Large amounts of fast-flowing water can cut similar channels in even hard rock, as in the Grand Canyon in North America.

## YOU DIG IT

Place a potted plant on a large clean sheet of paper. Sprinkle some water onto the plant from a height of two feet (60 cm). Are there any soil splatters on the paper? Repeat with a pot filled just with soil. How much soil splatter is on the paper now? Why the difference?

## NATURE'S UMBRELLA

The leaves of plants, particularly trees, protect the ground from heavy rainfalls. They act like an umbrella, stopping the rain splattering the ground underneath. Without them, a heavy rain can wash away the top layers of loose pebbles and soil.

▲ *Sea stacks on a coast*

## LOSING SUPPORT

✱ As rivers and streams cut into the rocks along their banks, they remove the support for the soil above. The soil falls into the water as a landslide. The rushing water carries away the loose material. Some of this scrapes away at the rock beneath, creating even deeper and wider valleys. Some loose soil gets dumped on the banks.

## ROCKY ISLANDS

Sea stacks are tall rock pillars found along coasts. They were once parts of seashore cliffs. The force of waves crashing against the cliffs caused weaker sections of rock to collapse. Harder rock sections have been left standing. These rocky islands, created by water erosion, are often homes to nesting birds.

# WIND AND ICE

**D**ry and cold regions of Earth are also shaped by erosion. Wind moves small particles quickly from place to place. Ice grinds slowly through mountains and can carry huge boulders long distances.

## BLOWING AWAY

Dust storms are caused by winds moving over dry land with little or no plant life protecting it. Small particles are picked up and carried high in the air. Unlike streams, wind is not limited to a river channel or waterway. It can carry its load over any landscape and set it down anywhere, too.

▼ *A dust storm whips up huge amounts of soil. It can darken the sky and cover anything in its path with a layer of particles.*

# ICE RIVERS

High in the mountains, snow packs down to form hard, thick ice. The weight of the ice causes it to start moving down the mountain like a slow, frozen river. This is a glacier. Along the way, the heavy ice digs up and carries along huge boulders and rocks. It also pushes soil and rock out of its way in front and to the sides, leaving mounds of dirt and rock on the land.

## YOU DIG IT

Blow on a pile of dry paper circles (hole paper punches) and then a pile of wet paper circles. Add a row of plants between you and the dry paper dots, then blow again. How do you explain the results?

## WAVES OF SAND

Desert sand is made of very fine, light particles. These are easily carried by the wind. A sandstorm can move whole sand dunes. Desert people need to find shelter from sand storms that can travel as fast as 80 miles an hour (130 km/h).

▼ *Sand dunes in North Africa*

▲ *A glacier eroding a mountain*

# ALL NATURAL EROSION

Erosion is happening all the time. It is nature's way of recycling material on Earth. Natural erosion helps to create valleys and **floodplains**. It also plays an important role in bringing nutrients to barren, or lifeless, areas.

## LAYER OF SEDIMENT

Flooding can cause a lot of damage to houses and property. But flooding can also work to improve soil. Floodplains are the flat lands on either side of a river. When the Nile River in Egypt floods, the minerals and nutrients carried in the water are deposited all along its banks. This makes the banks suitable for growing many kinds of crops. The Niger River in West Africa, the Ganges in Bangladesh, and the Missouri in the United States also have **fertile** floodplains.

## SOIL FACTS

✳ In Egypt about 3,500 years ago, farmers first learned how to irrigate their land. Irrigation is the **artificial** watering of soil. They dug channels in the floodplain then lifted water into them from the Nile using long poles with buckets on the end.

▶ *Serious flooding dumps mud on soil, killing plants and soil animals. The mud may have to be removed.*

# FERTILE FAN

The Nile River in Africa cuts through the dry Sahara Desert. As the river flows northward, it erodes particles of rocks from the riverbanks and river bottom. This thick sludge called **sediment** is carried along as the Nile slows on its way to the Mediterranean Sea. At the river mouth, the sediment is left behind creating a large delta, or triangle, of very fertile ground.

## NATURAL BEAUTY

Rocks erode at different rates. Rocks that are formed when layers of particles are cemented together under pressure are called sedimentary rocks. They erode much faster than harder rocks such as granite or marble. Wind and water can erode sedimentary rock and leave arches or bridges of hard rock.

▶ Rock arches

# THE HUMAN EFFECT

There is a balance in nature between land that is eroded and land that is made by **deposition**. Humans often upset the balance. Farming, logging, and construction can all make erosion worse.

## ALL CHOKED UP

The Mississippi River carries a lot of sediment into the Gulf of Mexico. Irrigation adds water to soil that may already be soaked with rainwater. This causes soil to be washed away much quicker than just by heavy rains. The Mississippi River Delta becomes **clogged** or choked with sediment. Today, the Delta is growing into the Gulf by about six miles (10 km) every century.

▶ *In June 2008, part of the Mississippi flooded its banks causing serious damage to local farming communities.*

*▼ Too many grazing sheep in an area can destroy grassland.*

# COUNTING SHEEP

Cattle, sheep, and other livestock need a lot of grass. They graze seven to 12 hours a day. If pastures are not allowed to regrow between **grazing**, they can become bare. Bare soil does not have a strong network of roots to hold it in place. It is easily blown or washed away.

## TOO MUCH IS NO GOOD

Irrigation is useful only if the water has a chance to gradually soak into the soil. If land is watered too much, nutrients can be washed out of the soil, leaving it useless for plants to grow. If the water falls fast on sun-baked or tightly packed soil, it runs off so fast that it has hardly any benefit.

## SOIL FACTS

✻ Some farmers irrigate their land from pipes buried in the soil. The pipes have tiny holes in them that allows water to trickle out.

*▲ Irrigating a field*

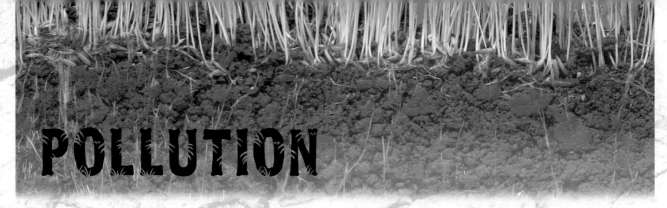

# POLLUTION

Soil naturally has a mix of chemicals. If people add chemicals to soil, accidently or deliberately, they can kill plants, soil micro life, and animals that feed on them.

Pollution is the adding of unwanted chemicals to land, water, or air. All pollution can poison soil.

◄ This small airplane is spraying chemicals on a field.

## AIR ATTACK!

Airplanes are used to spray large areas of soil with **fertilizers** and chemicals that control weeds and insects. The chemicals are **absorbed** slowly into the ground. A strong wind can pick up the top layer of soil with the chemicals and blow it somewhere else. It may fall on fields that are not used for crops. Helpful insects or wild grasses can be wiped out.

## LANDFILL

Chemicals can sometimes get into the ground by accident. Dumping garbage in landfill sites, traffic accidents, or spillages at factories can lead to toxins, or poisons, seeping into the soil. If the soil is not cleaned up quickly, a heavy rainfall or a landslide can spread the pollution. Once pollution is on the move, it is much harder to clean up.

▼ *A domestic landfill*

## YOU DIG IT

Set a funnel in the mouth of a jar. Line it with a coffee filter paper. Mix three cups (0.70L) of soil with powdered red paint. Put the colored soil in the filter paper. Now pour three (0.70L) cups of water slowly into the soil. The red powdered paint is like pollution in the soil. See how much of the pollution is carried away by the water.

## SOIL FACTS

✳ Scientists often take samples of soil to test the levels of pollutants in them. Some soils are so toxic that they must be burned.

◀ *Testing polluted water*

# IMPACT ON WILDLIFE

Erosion plays a big part in the survival of wildlife. Both plants and animals depend on healthy soil for food and living areas. Where erosion is unchecked, wildlife struggles to survive. Any changes in wildlife can affect humans, too.

## TOPSOIL COMMUNITY

As plants and animals die and decay, nutrients are returned to the soil. Soil that stays in place over a long period of time becomes very fertile. The healthy topsoil can support a wide variety of plants and a **thriving** community of micro life. This attracts all kinds of larger animals, both plant- and meat-eaters.

## MEDICINE BARK

Many plants provide us with useful medicinal chemicals. The Pacific Yew is a type of evergreen tree. It has a thin, scaly, brown bark. Scientists have discovered chemicals in its bark that can be used to make a drug that helps fight cancer. The Pacific Yew is a threatened species. If the soil in which it grows is not protected, it might die out.

▲ *A scientist takes samples from tree bark*

## CUT DOWN IN SIZE

Rain forests provide more food, shelter, and oxygen for animals than any other **habitat**, or living area, on Earth. They also remove lots of carbon dioxide gas from the air. This helps reduce **global warming**. But many rain forests are being cut down for timber or to make room for farmland. Their destruction should be limited.

### SOIL FACTS

✳ Each year an area of rain forest twice the size of Florida is destroyed by humans.

▶ Rain forests in Southeast Asia are home to the orangutan.

21

# EFFECTS ON HUMANS

Humans are also affected by soil erosion and damage. Loss of soil, poor farming, and soil pollution can cause problems with our food and water supplies.

## CLEAN WATER

✳ Sixty percent of our body is made of water. Clean drinking water is vital to our health. Erosion and pollution can lead to more sediment and chemicals ending up in our water supply. Clean, fresh water is also important for livestock and crops. If cattle and crops are given polluted water, the chemicals will find their way into our food.

◀ In this village in West Africa, people get fresh water from a well deep in the ground. If the surrounding soil gets polluted, in time the well will be, too, and the villagers will become ill.

## FISH NURSERY

Too much sediment or silt in a river can cause problems with the fish that we eat such as rainbow trout and sockeye salmon. These fish spawn, or lay their eggs, in gravelly river beds. They return year after year to the same spot. Too much sediment or silt can bury the gravel. The fish will not spawn in a muddy area, which means large populations will die off.

## SNACK TIME

A favorite food of many types of fish that we eat are stoneflies and mayflies. These insects live in or near fresh water. They are both **sensitive** to pollution. Chemicals washed out of soil by rain or irrigation can find their way into rivers and kill them. If these insects are found in or around a lake, pond, or stream, it is a sign of good quality water. Scientists regularly check water quality.

▲ *Scientists check water quality regularly.*

# STOP IT

**H**umans can slow down or stop much of soil erosion. They can do this by improving how they farm, build, and use the world around them.

▼ *A man points at mudslide damage to his house following a severe storm in Taiwan in August 2009. The soil around his house was easily eroded due to poor construction work.*

## BALANCING ACT

Flooding is nature's way of returning nutrients and minerals to the land. By building floodwalls and **levees**, people prevent this cycle from happening. People need to allow floods to happen but in a controlled way. Also, they should not build homes or industries on floodplains. This can lead to soil loss and pollution.

## YOU DIG IT

Grow some little plants in a soil tray until they have made roots. Fill another soil tray with just soil. In the bottom of a plastic or Styrofoam cup, make several holes. Fill the cup with water and make it "rain" on both soil trays. What happens to each soil? Now make the holes in the cup bigger to create heavy rain. Tilt the trays up slightly and "rain" on them again. What do you see now?

▲ Chesapeake Bay sea wall

# HOLDING BACK WATER

Humans can also help areas likely to have erosion problems by building walls. Retention walls hold back soil and rocks. They can reduce the bad effects construction work or water has on the landscape.

## LIMITED USE

Plant roots hold soil in place. By cutting down trees carefully and only when needed, soil can be protected. Planting marram grass in sand dunes can stop winds blowing the sand away and enrich sandy soils. Forests on slopes or riverbanks can be left in place to avoid landslides. Livestock can be allowed to graze at only certain times of year, to allow grass to regrow. Houses can be built with gardens all around, not concreted areas.

# BETTER FARMING

**F**armers plow soil to turn it over, bringing buried nutrients to the surface. Plowing also helps air and water flow through the soil, breaking up the hard surface of topsoil. Farmers drill holes in the soil to sow seeds and plants.

▼ *In China, rice is grown on mountain terraces.*

## DOWNHILL

Soil on sloping ground is easily eroded as gravity can pull everything downhill. By plowing in lines that run along or across the slopes and not down, rainwater runs away more slowly. This gives it more time to seep into the ground. This is called contour plowing, named after the lines drawn on a map joining places of the same height above sea level.

## SOIL FACTS

✳ Vegetables often do well without fertilizers if planted in small areas between trees and not in huge fields. The trees enrich the soil with nutrients and prevent soil erosion.

## NO-TILL FARMING

Farmers are learning ways to disturb the soil less when planting. No-till farming means new crops are planted without digging out all old crop stems and roots. Scientists have found soil creatures do best if not constantly disturbed. A covering of old crops stops wind and rain from eroding the soil.

▼ *No-till farming*

▼ *A vegetable garden*

# HOW YOU CAN HELP

**W**e must all take part in reducing erosion. It is not just the job of farmers, builders, or scientists. By changing what food we buy, what we eat, and how we **dispose** of our waste, we can protect the soil.

## WASTE TO COMPOST

Composting is a way to turn kitchen scraps into a natural fertilizer. Micro life in a compost bin breaks down vegetable peelings, fruit skins, and eggshells into nutrients and minerals. Adding compost to soil helps plants grow healthy root systems. It binds soil together so there is less wind and water erosion and helps dry soils take up water.

◄ *Composting is one way you can have a positive effect on soil.*

# GOOD FOR YOU!

Farming methods that protect the environment are good for us, too. Organic farmers do not use any artificial fertilizers or chemical pest and weed controls on their fields. Plants that help bring nutrients into the soil, along with insect predators, are used to maintain the health of the soil. We can support these good farming practices by buying organic food.

## RECYCLING

We can all help in preventing erosion. Recycling paper and cans and reusing old furniture reduces the need for wood and metals. Fewer logging sites and mines mean less soil is disturbed cutting down trees or digging pits. Planting trees and bushes slows the effects of wind and rain on the soil. By not concreting over gardens and yards, you are allowing rain to seep into the ground naturally rather than collect and run away in floods.

▶ *Collect household waste for recycling.*

29

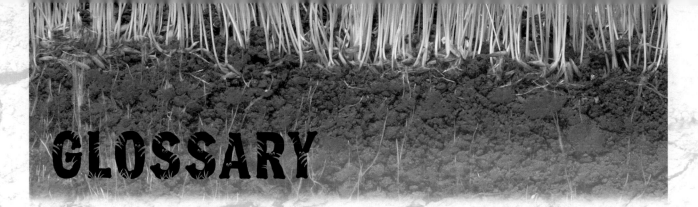

# GLOSSARY

**absorb** To take, or suck, something in

**artificial** Made by humans; not natural

**bacteria** Tiny living things made of a single cell

**clogged** Choked or stopped up

**crops** Plants grown to provide food and useful materials such as cotton

**deposition** Collected sediment being dropped or dumped

**dispose** Throw or give away

**erosion** Wearing away

**fertile** Soil rich in nutrients so that crops can be grown

**fertilizers** Chemicals added to soil to improve plant growth

**floodplains** Low, level land next to rivers that is often flooded

**glacier** A slowlymoving mass of ice

**global warming** A gradual increase in Earth's temperature

**grazing** Feeding on the plants in a meadow

**gullies** Ditches or channels formed by fast-flowing water

**habitat** The environment where organisms live

**landslide** A movement of a mass of loose earth

**levee** A mound along a riverbank that is built to prevent flooding

**lichens** Organisms of fungi and algae living together as one

**mature** Fully developed

**minerals** Useful chemicals in rocks

**mountain building** The Earth's plates piling into each other, pushing up mountains

**nutrients** Substances used for energy; food

**organic** Made from/by living things

**organism** Any living thing

**sediment** A mass of small particles carried along by flowing water

**sensitive** Reacts easily

**silt** Mud; a thick paste of particles

**thriving** Growing well

**unstable** Easily moved

**weathering** Rocks or stones broken down by wind, rain, and ice

# MORE INFORMATION

## FURTHER READING

*Composting: Nature's Recyclers*. Robin Koontz. Picture Window
    Books, 2007
*Erosion*. Joelle Riley. Lerner Publications, 2006
*Erosion: Changing Earth's Surface*. Robin Koontz. Picture Window
    Books, 2007
*Soil! Get the Inside Scoop*. David Lindbo. American Society of
    Agronomy, 2008
*What Shapes the Land?* Bobbie Kalman. Crabtree Publishing
Company, 2009

## WEB SITES

**Rader's Geography4Kids!:**
www.geography4kids.com/
**The Dirt on Soil:**
http://school.discoveryeducation.com/schooladventures/soil/
**Protecting Your Property From Erosion:**
www.abag.ca.gov/bayarea/enviro/erosion/erosion.html
**Natural Resources Conservation Service:**
www.nrcs.usda.gov/feature/education/squirm/skworm.html
**Soil for Schools:**
www.soil-net.com/legacy/schools/index.htm

# INDEX